**Anyone Left Standing**

To my mother

**Previous publications:**
*Waiting for the Morning* (a novel) ( The Women's Press, 1991)
*The Little Book of Lice* (1998)
Short stories in magazines and broadcast on Radio 4

Acknowledgements are due to the editors of the following publications: *Dancing the Tightrope* (The Women's Press 1987), *In the Pink* (The Women's Press 1983), *The North, One Foot on the Mountain, Overdraft, Smiths Knoll, The West in her Eye* (Pyramid Press 1995)

*Anyone Left Standing* was the winning collection in The Poetry Business Book & Pamphlet Competition 1997

# Anyone Left Standing

Kath Mckay

*Smith/Doorstop Books*

Published 1998 by
Smith/Doorstop Books
The Poetry Business
The Studio
Byram Arcade
Westgate
Huddersfield HD1 1ND

Copyright © Kath Mckay
All Rights Reserved

Kath Mckay hereby asserts her moral right to be identified as the author of this book.

ISBN 1-902382-05-6

British Library Cataloguing-in-Publication Data. A catalogue record for this book is available from the British Library.

Typeset at The Poetry Business
Printed by Peepal Tree Press, Leeds
Cover picture by Bob Moulder

Distributed by Littlehampton Book Services Ltd, 10-14 Eldon Way, Lineside Estate, Littlehampton BN17 7HE

The Poetry Business gratefully acknowledges the help of Kirklees Metropolitan Council and Yorkshire & Humberside Arts.

## CONTENTS

| | |
|---|---|
| 7 | Gold |
| 8 | On being Massaged |
| 9 | Escape |
| 10 | Dreams |
| 11 | Van Gogh and the Pointillists |
| 12 | Emergency Dentist |
| 13 | Anyone Left Standing |
| 14 | Eating Popcorn |
| 15 | Eight O'clock, First Day |
| 16 | Spanish Omelette |
| 17 | Ground Cover Genus Vinca |
| 18 | First Aid |
| 19 | Roman sisters, Vindolanda, Northumbria: A.D. 100 |
| 20 | Maggie |
| 21 | High over Asphalt |
| 22 | Goldfish |
| 24 | Chinese Mushrooms |
| 25 | Hamburgers With or Without |
| 26 | Extra Time |
| 27 | Winter Day |
| 28 | Stocktaking |
| 29 | Arthur Flying at Eighty |
| 30 | Rats in Italy |
| 31 | But the Teeth? |
| 32 | She Happens to Know |
| 33 | Father's Day 1970 |
| 35 | Tap Roots |
| 36 | Breakwater |
| 37 | The Sandwich |
| 38 | Still Life |
| 39 | Names |
| 40 | Other Things |
| 41 | View of the Pond |
| 42 | To My Mother |
| 43 | Funeral at Easter |

| | |
|---|---|
| 44 | No More |
| 45 | Two Cappuccino and a Tuna Fish Sandwich |
| 46 | Internet |
| 47 | Creating |
| 48 | Umbrellas |
| 49 | Dun Laoghaire |
| 50 | When we moved from London |
| 51 | Going Home |
| 53 | Nearly There |
| 54 | Differences |
| 55 | To Phil (if he wakes up) |

# *Gold*

I am following instruction and Mrs Oakley
at the Tottenham Court Road branch of Sight and Sound
is going on about a, s, semi colon, l,
and how you have to get your home keys right
or you will never develop good habits.
Uphill in Kensal Green Cemetery
the leaves on Taxus baccata fastigiata aureomaginata
edge with yellow. My skin feels itchy from not seeing the sun,
the back of my shirt grows moist. Typewriter keys get hot,
ink smells sharp as vodka. The quick brown fox jumps.
A ballerina tells me as she bites into a Kit Kat
that she never eats meals. Crunchy bars, coke,
an occasional banana; 'It doesn't pay to get fat.'
Teenage Kicks plays on the radio. When I close my eyes,
shavings of gold leaf float towards me.

## On being Massaged

I like this deep touch, this digging in,
this pummelling out of things.
Mapping my back, North East is my father;
a train, a quick kiss, a promise,
the smell of tobacco on his breath,
his hand on my shoulder.
Scheveningen station. A beach, a walk on the promenade.
Smoke rising from houses. And cows.
Breathing, I see breath.

North West my mother waits, speaking French.
Wears stockings, Chanel. Under her coat are bones.
She brushes my cheeks lightly, tells me I have to be a big girl.
'Daddy will be home soon.' So we wait. Several months. Years.
There are noises in the night and the crops in the fields fail,
soldiers' boots tramp over cabbages. In England
a woman gives me sausage.
My mother holds my sweaty hand,
as we step down to meet a skeleton of a man.
He cries 'my little angelina' and goes to kiss me.
Three brown teeth stick out from his old man's face.
I do not like this daddy I have been given,
but when he puts his hand on my shoulders,
I remember North East and the feel of his fingers.

## *Escape*

It began when Ruth up at the main road
forgot to keep hold of the skateboard and it started rolling,
fast down the alley, past the acupuncturist with red geraniums,
past Doctor Sayed, who never makes appointments,
the ex-councillor whose son feeds him with information,
Russian vine covering his fence. Past the planning notice
for an extension, the two German shepherd dogs,
the boat and the caravan that never move,
the van on bricks, the greenhouse with each window smashed,
raw grapes spreading like a fungus,
past the family with ten kids and the mattresses growing
in the backyard, Julia who's just had a baby and is moving,
Karen who's having a baby and isn't moving.
'My dad died in a waterfall' Karen's daughter claimed last year;
now he's surfaced, Karen's belly has grown fat.
Past the garages where the kids go in for a smoke,
the woman carpenter, the man who fixes motorbikes,
the kids who ripped off his batteries,
the women's centre with its sauna,
the Asian youths who do Tai Chi at night
to try and beat its infra red alarm,
Mr Kim who stores up baskets, newspapers, shop dummies,
plants he has rescued from the park.
Says he's a Vietnamese agent,
distributes Fortune Cookies every Chinese New Year.
At the bottom of the alley, Sandra sings Puccini.
The high notes reach out through windows.
In front of the Holy Trinity, a bride steps out of a car;
'You is all Jesus' disciples', says the vicar,
as the skateboard crashes into a NACRO hut.
Wood splinters, the undercarriage flies off.
Children scatter. The bride looks alarmed.

## *Dreams*

Ali dreams of Mecca, as he sits
in the brown B reg Montego
outside his front door.
He has learnt the names of things. Clutch. Accelerator. Brake.
Some days his brother arrives in a red Peugeot
and takes him to school, where others laugh at him
and point to their heads. His father travels twice a year to Mecca
and, of the leaking gutter, says the Corporation will provide.
Ali asks his sister Naseema, who are the Corporation?
but she shrugs her shoulders, eyes their mother's belly,
fat again now, clears betel nuts from the yard.

## Van Gogh and the Pointillists

It's always the same, but different, the ones who let you in.
That painting of the crying girl on the wall,
spider plants in the window, digestive biscuits.
Stories about their husband, how he fought in Greece,
children doing well. Grandchildren?
Expensive to New Zealand. A pause.
'I like paintings. Joined the council scheme.
I've had Van Gogh, and the pointillists.
What about you?'
They refill my cup while I explain how
there's an 'internationally respected team of artists
working round the clock to fulfil orders;
based in Middlesex, near the airport actually,' how
'art adds to your life, can be a good investment
... a range of insurance packages
for total peace of mind.'

'Do you have one with butterflies?'

We've almost finished Brent Cross now.
Every time we pass the shopping centre,
I see a trolley left in the road.
On the way back to Camden, Sharukh says
if people want to buy paintings, it's our job to sell them.
Otherwise, how will I pay for next term? A Trotskyist,
Sharukh claims working in a Clerkenwell toilet
has taught him more than LSE. We argue
whether we should be honest with the customers.
Next day I get the sack. Mrs Cohen at 36 Dickson Drive
complained I told her the paintings weren't worth
the paper they were painted on. She already had three.

## Emergency Dentist

These are my instruments; long, flat, cold.
A probe, a pick, a mini-vacuum, a drill. This is my room.
A wrecker's yard of casts and moulds, the smell of mouthwash.
Pink. I can make you whole, fuse bone with metal, mercury.
Canine, molar, incisor.

Always you come on Sunday afternoons, when pubs have shut
and fathers take children for rides in the park.
Skateboards fly, wheels grow wobbly, roller blades skew.
My door is open, a breeze blows through.
Pre-molar. Milk teeth. Wisdom.

I take a film and stop and pin. Splint and fill.
Inject, pile on and build your eaters and chewers.
But sometimes the pectinated edge of a second tooth
will make me cry. My glue is strong, but roots do die.
Crown. Extract. Bridge. Plate.

I have two daughters. At six and eight,
they're always moving. Up and down. Along. Beside.
I want that they should keep their mouths shut
but take more photos of full smiles.
Now I say open. Wounds will heal. Evening passes.
Grinders, gnashers, front teeth, back teeth.

## *Anyone Left Standing*

She never did like apples, because of her teeth.
The top ones didn't fit properly after the operation.
'Double murder' is her favourite ice cream;
two chocolate flakes. Pleased she can eat it.
Same with the wheelchair. 'At this level,' she says
'you notice new buds and night scented stock.'
On our first wheeled outing, 22 kids
from the special school
are also pushed to the park.
Everyone waves, and anyone left standing looks odd.
She was kneeling in front of the record player
when her leg went. Now in the photos she shows me,
my mother floats on clouds; with her bad eye
and shaky hands, all images double exposed.
Her sitting on the patio, the high rise drifting behind.
A neighbour twenty foot up. Smells better up there.

## *Eating Popcorn*

It's evening, late July, and we lie with our toes in cold grit
on the foreshore of the River Kuban. Grey powder floats
and, when you breathe in, hurts your lungs and eyes.
Today we have skipped classes, Linda and Arthur and I.
Ignored our history tutor and twenty million dead.
You get sick of suffering. I prefer the sun
struggling through smog. No matter. We dangle our toes.
Fat women in flowery swimming costumes
shout at each other, eat black bread and oranges.
A man in an overcoat swigs vodka.
Linda sips at Pepsi, asks why the Russians don't wake up
to the benefits of capitalism. She misses the bin.
'Debushka' shouts a woman; a hand clamps my shoulder.
Meekly we place the bottle. As we leave,
we notice on boards behind glass
inked-in pictures of mother heroes, workers
who've 'exceeded their norm', copies of Pravda, Isvestia.
But no rusty dodgems, ice-cream stalls, greasy caffs,
no eating popcorn. Only grey sand, a factory making smoke.
A small patch of green.

## *Eight O'clock, First Day,*

                Pilar brings me tea.
Silently, we put on sandals which bind our feet,
head down to the beach. On the sand
bright sails are pinned against rocks.
Tanned men in tight wetsuits limber up,
busy themselves with ropes. Behind us,
Teide, mist on its slopes.
The sun's obscured by clouds, but it'll be hot.

'Italian', Pilar says, 'small bums'.
Before the beach becomes theirs, we're in the water.
Nothing prepares me for the warmth, the salt foam,
seaweed that wreaths my ankles. I'm pale in black,
she's topless and brown, hair turned to ringlets.
And she sings. We dive into wave after wave.
Each one slaps our bellies, pushing us breathless down.
We swim to deep water. Pilar opens her throat.
Nothing before Africa.

A surfer cuts close to our legs; we surface to land.
Always before, we've been friends set in concrete;
dog shit on pavements, Mondays at the Rio,
rooting in Oxfam. A trickle of water between us:
Hackney Baths, the Regent's Canal,
the grey empty Thames. Now we've got extra:
The Atlantic, El Médano, El Teide, El Mar.

## Spanish Omelette

'I will not have that cheap soya.'
Sunflower oil, Marisa demands. Girasol.
Then the onions. Spanish of course. Cut them in rings.
Fry slowly until not quite done.
Salt the potatoes, slice wafer thin.
Have them pile up. Fry in the same oil.
'And now for the secret,' she says.
'Only the Spanish know this.'
Mash the potatoes, a little. It's a cake, remember.'
Fork in the eggs. No water. You must have no water.
Mix. Add one gas ring. Marisa's bad temper.
Her flying arms. Mice skitting across floors.
A great sun. Salsa singer in the square.
Hips waving. Ships to Venezuela.

## *Ground Cover Genus Vinca*

Dark green that first year, it lacked promise,
huddled against the wall. Nettles rioted over it,
white and choking. Butterflies hovered, bees
got their fill. But we dug and cleared, found out its name:
periwinkle. Ground cover, 'useful where weeds'.
By it I placed a cauldron yanked up from the cellar,
filled it with pansies. This year its green became brighter,
shot all over, shy purple flowers nudged out into the sun.
Free now, covering distances.
Ground cover. Making ground.

## *First Aid*

Strange how the shape of my blood on the sheet
mirrors what we have just done – you hanging down in
and then out of me. Like an ink blot, a Rorschach test.
First on the scene, you bring tissue. Handkerchiefs. Cold water.
Clean off the evidence.

# Roman sisters, Vindolanda, Northumbria: A.D. 100

*Vale soror anima mea ita valeam.*
farewell my sister, my dearest soul
*Karissima et have*
as I hope to prosper and hail.

Outside, in the wind, men shift supplies, clerks write
lists of vegetables soldiers are to eat, while Claudia Severa
scratches out a birthday invite to Sulpicia Lepidina.
Later, as an empire crumbles and garrisons flee,
lists so carefully formed will be set on fire.
But flames die quickly in peat
and the words will stay fixed as photographs
till one day in 1988 an archeologist will find them,
along with this, the first letter found in Western Europe,
from one woman to another. Claudia tells her slave
to get the children ready, as they are to eat. Life is short,
in this place they call home, but tempered by honey
and good meat. Today there is rabbit.
Her husband Aelius has to drill the men.
Aelius has lines round his eyes. She forgets
how long he has soldiered, but knows that few men
last till grey hair. She sees the first wisps
round his ears, pulls the children to her. Seals her letter.
Warns her slave not to buy fish sauce:
the quality is uncertain, as the journey across Europe
is long. Time for decay and besides, she cannot bear to taste it,
for through it she remembers colours and warm nights,
the cry of traders in the market, boats, the start of their journey.

*The opening salutation was written by Claudia Severa herself, rather than by a scribe, and she was, according to the museum, a 'diabolical writer'; hence the misspelling of 'Carissima'.*

## *Maggie*

Maggie lives on Cathedral View. If she stands on the bed.
Among the GCSE files, a skull: 'Remember where we're going.'
On the shelves *Women who Love Too Much*,
*Gargantua and Pantagruel, Improving your Driving.*
Muddy Waters. On the wall, 'The Hand that Rocks the Cradle',
John and Yoko in New York. 'Nothing changed
except we all dressed up a bit.'
Maggie's neutered tortoiseshell crawls over the bowl
of decomposing pears. Ellen next door
thinks Maggie's not quite respectable.
Can't put her finger on it.
Each day Maggie drives off in teacher clothes,
but there was that night last summer,
a man roared up on a Norton.
The look on Maggie's face. Didn't see her for four days.
'Please feed the cat', said the note.
Always passes the time of day. Off to Manchester soon
on a Balti course. 'Lovely weather'.
Waters her lettuces on a Saturday.
Wears a sarong.

## *High over Asphalt*

We're stuffed with chocolate when John from two doors down
wraps our tree, first in scaffolding, tied in a triangle
round its trunk, like Christo wrapping the Reichstag.
Then in green cloth, and red, to bind the poles.
He lashes boards with twine for a platform twelve foot up,
calls it a treehouse. Kids perch,
high over asphalt. It looks like an army spy post
in West Belfast. Margaret says we could fill in the gaps
with plastic, hang flowering baskets.
I wonder about planning permission.
'Looks great,' shouts a passing acupuncturist,
as John drives in a nail.

The holidays end, we decide to take it down.
Teenagers might spit on the cars,
spy on our opposite neighbour as she sunbathes
nude. John looks murderously angry.
Two days it took him to put up this structure
for his fortnightly children and others
who want to go high. That night I dream of him,
a sniper in the open sided treehouse.
His son falls off into thick black mud.
John dives to save him, comes up for air.

## *Goldfish*

Today I picked nits from my daughter's head
and a bomb went off at South Quays.
A mouse moved across the floor,
slow now, poisoned by the Council.
On the phone, my mother said 'Jeezus, I don't know'
when I asked about the tumour in her ear.
'I have to go, it's the nurses' phone'.
My daughter wanted to know what I did in work
what happened downstairs after she'd gone to sleep
and what was my favourite colour pen.
Red.
And then when I sat at the table and cried,
and gave two reasons for being sad,
she said you can't get sad for two reasons,
if you're already sad from one.
Today my son was eighteen and we celebrated.
Pizza they wouldn't deliver because their drivers get mugged,
Veuve Aubin, Tesco, £3.99, gets better by the glassful.
He took his share to his room.
I thought we should burn something or snip a knot,
but I fell asleep reading about a man called Sunset.
Worked in a bar, was always travelling west.
Today, my twelve year old said what he hated most about me
was my nosiness and I thought that soon my mother,
with her first floor view of the Post Office,
might have a hole in the side of her head.
Today cold rain spat against the windows,
fat green shoots pushed up through the last of the snow
and I learnt that imbolc means the time before spring
when light increases and days lengthen,
and that people in Headingley do a dance about it.
Today Deirdre McAliskey and Jonathon Taylor
both stood for President of Queen's University, Belfast.
Twenty years on from their parents,
they look out from the paper, clear eyes, curly hair.

'My politics are my own', she says,
while not denying her republican socialist background.
He concentrates on the removal of Irish language signs
                                    from the Union.
Today there is only a crust left on my daughter's eyelid
where Herpes Simplex burrowed in for two weeks.
Today we bought a goldfish.
'Maybe it's lonely', said my daughter,
so Raymond Chandler's *Goldfish*,
with its Penguin 60s cover,
glistens behind the bowl.

## Chinese Mushrooms

The night before, five of us ate chinese mushrooms,
while red paper dragons fell to the floor.
Black fungi glistened on my plate like sea anemones.

Next day, my mother's a lop-sided moonface
crude stitches stapled onto the dough
taken from her shoulder. Undersea fronds
cut off now, eustachian tube drains back on itself.

A theatre mob-cap on her small shaven skull.
'I'll be getting a wig. I fancy a red one,
and I'm down for new glasses.'
She perches the old pair on the rise of her face.
'If they put a false ear on the end, they'll stay on.'

'You'll be hearing in mono now,'
says my brother, filling in gaps.
'Yeah, a stereo's no use.' She's holding her stitches.
As we hoot, others howl from their beds.

Over the Pennines, we're blasted by Kurt Cobain.
'I'd kill myself if I looked like that'.
My son goes on about changing the car
'Crap car. Old'. Another overtakes. He becomes quiet.
Across the valley a shrunken red car, make unknown,
slips along the side of a snowcapped hill.

## Hamburgers With or Without

While the glamorous granny contest goes on next door,
Mullin fries a hamburger special;
beef, onions, tomatoes, gherkins.
Ketchup extra. I hide Lorca under the till.
The afternoon grinds on. Blue meanies pounce.
Rumours fly: 'They caught someone last night.
Fantasy Island, three in the morning.'
Nothing seems real. Mungo Jerry on the radio,
grannies who lost in for a coffee,
say the winner's got false teeth, a fake tan, addled legs.
I read about The Poet in New York, while Mullin looks me over.
He's doing politics at Aston, but says that's all theory.
This is real life. He smells of grease and cigarettes.
'Still on for tonight?' I blush, and later when we meet,
me in the long blue dress I feel stupid in, conversation dries up.
With puffed sleeves, the dress skirts my ankles.
We can't even cycle to the pub. 'What's wrong with you?'
He tells me to change: 'The less you have on,
the quicker it'll come off.'

But something makes me want to wear it. Girls on dates
wear dresses like this. His eyes are green and laughing
and his hand's up my skirt.

On the beach someone plucks a guitar.
We've got all August in this place. We talk of revolution,
how Pontins shouldn't employ students
because they undercut the local workers.
He analyses the situation in the North of Ireland: 'Basically,
the working classes of the Protestant and Catholic communities
need to unite against their common oppressors'.
But his hand's up my skirt.
Later blue meanies run along the corridor,
flashing their torches, flushing us out.

## Extra Time

The terrain is different now. No signposts.
A different ballgame on this post-vasectomy field.
Codpiece hung up to dry like a one breasted bra,
small line of bumps across your balls,
stitches gathered together. Tiny threads
dissolve in the baths you oh so gingerly take.
Containers labelled 'semen' wait to be filled
in three months' time.

'You're my last baby', you say to our daughter,
as you snuggle down to read, her wide-cheekboned face
next to yours. 'Don't die', you say, a catch in your throat.
'I'll try not to', she laughs. Regret crawls over the house.
Never, it says, never, never again.
Old age and emptiness. The pitch bare.

It's midsummer, next door shouts fly
through open windows, as Ireland lose to Mexico.
They have the barbecue anyway. Smoke curls
before the storm sends lightning shivers across the park.
Children throw basketballs high in the air
the scent of honeysuckle wafts across, mixed with dog.

Glastonbury. We watch on late TV, and sweat.
Somewhere inside a memory's loosed,
and lust comes unannounced, like after childbirth,
slow falling into each other's arms,
slow suck of flesh on flesh, no barriers.
We know now why your balls were tweaked and pulled.

And part of me can't believe
we're entitled to this.

## Winter Day

Later, in the park on this mild November day,
in the quiet time before schools let out,
only a few people with dogs,
I'm suddenly happy because I'm not dead.

I try to remember
the way I thought it strange a health campaigner
should drive the few streets to my house;
how she grilled vegi-burgers at the school barbecue;
her in a cold East London hall, doing Tai Chi
at nine thirty in the morning;
the argument we had about my article.

And all the time something nags –
How old are her children? The obituary says they 'flourished'
at the comprehensive she believed in.
Older than mine, I remember. It's then it gets to me,
as the first parents make their way across the path;
while inside children put on coats, collect their bags,
the time before hometime.

## Stocktaking

42 not out. Three children, one grown,
half a house, unfinished. A man I've known for years,
words on a page. A houseful of books. Friends.
A diary often filled. Things to do in the day.
A few trips to Italy and the States. Still got my teeth.
Hip gets a bit stiff when I don't have sex.
A tendency to ear infections. Sometimes I can't sleep.
Womb intact at the moment. But pressures will build.
Bank balance tipping. Haven't paid the bills.

Then a letter tells me
her husband knocked her front teeth out
and she left in the night with the kids.

Last day of the summer term she's just come top in Art.
The teacher says she should go to college,
but she's pregnant and no, she won't do her O levels,
'For Jimmy wouldn't like it'.

Looking at the picture now, us with our long skinny legs,
our straight brushed hair, mini-skirts riding up our thighs,
I want to close the gap, hand out blessings like a priest.
She adds she's studying computers. Should never have married him.
The divorce is on its way. Pleased I've done well.

We apologise for the inconvenience
while stocktaking takes place.
We hope to resume normal service as soon as possible.
In the meantime, here is some music.

# Arthur Flying at Eighty

'C'est merveilleux', he says in Elementary French.
Present tense. Future and past come later.
Monday morning, first class after the holidays,
marooned in a portacabin in a sea of mud.
So cold we keep our coats on.
Marie's asking what presents we got for Christmas,
did we do anything exciting? 'A CD,' 'A book,'
'Je regarde la télévision.' 'Pour le noel,' says Arthur,
'et pour mon anniversaire quatre vingt
my wife bought me a flight in a small plane.
Wetherby, Otley, Burley, Huddersfield, Ilkley –
we went all over. Five miles from the airport and ...'
'En français, Artur,' says Marie. 'Le pilote me dit –
See that red light – that's Leeds-Bradford. Go for it!'
The skin falls away from his face.
'So I took control.' Eyes brighten. 'C'est merveilleux.
I want to go up again. And when I came back,' he adds,
'my wife said I looked like ...' 'En français, Artur.'
'Un petit garçon.' 'Quel homme!' we shout.
All morning we're gliding.

## Rats in Italy

Each morning, we walked through the village for bread
pulled from big ovens by old women in black shawls;
the smell drew us from the observatory in the hills
where Sam plotted stars. Outside a craggy lunar landscape
made everything giant – snails, sunflowers, blackberries.
At night we ate pasta, tomatoes, olives big as stones,
at weekends roasted meat on the rocks. The men we called Luigi
stuck. Twelve 'ragazze belle' from Ireland, rare
in Castelgrande, Potenza. One day we felt queasy,
vomited on waking. 'The change of food, the climate,'
said Sam. 'The water.' In the barrel three fat, huddled rats;
pelts smoothed, the smell of decay. Water stained yellow.
Easy to see that once they fell in, they couldn't get out.
We buried the rats, refilled the barrel, each night inspected it.
Continued to buy bread.

## *But the Teeth?*

The day we met at the bus stop you said your father
was 'stable but dying' and we laughed, holding our sides,
staring at the young men in puffy sports jackets
and boats for trainers milling outside the Hayfield pub
and the children vexing their parents for Cantor's cod and chips
and the Anglican nuns carrying Ruth Rendell. You said
you'd read all the crime books in Chapeltown library.
Time to move on.
'It's his false teeth she's most worried about.
We can give away the clothes. But the teeth?'
And stable but dying we got on the bus
and stable but dying we went to town.
November and the Christmas lights already on.
I did my shopping, caught *The Big Sleep* on TV
as people still waited outside the bookies
for their number to come up.

## She Happens to Know

that light travels in straight lines
dark shadows form behind objects that get in light's way,
the furthest stars are already gone before we see them,
glass is transparent and people opaque and that light
can go round the world eight times in one second.
'What is light?' she asks, as crows pick off detritus in the park,
I know what it does, but what is it?' I tell her
matter is made up of very small particles,
that Outer Space is totally dark because no dust or water
reflects light. A magpie hops on a bin.
'Two thirds of the universe we have not seen'.
A park keeper sweeps up oak leaves, sycamore.
We hunch deeper into our coats.
'How do straight things like buses go round corners?'
I'm trying to explain about wheels, when the last sun
floods high-rises somewhere near Killingbeck,
turning windows and concrete to gold.

## Father's Day 1970

This is the day my father lets us sleep, then brings us tea in bed. The sun streams in at unusual angles. He leaves his docker's hook among the coats, and his gasbag empty, like a small dead animal.'Come on,' he says *'el día libre.'* My mother joins him. Perched on our bed, they laugh together as if they're younger. 'Let's go', he says. 'We'll miss the train.' My mother's eyes scale cupboards, hands twitch, as she plans out a meal. 'Potatoes and carrot.' I see her lips move. 'We need some eggs.' Like King Canute, he stops her. 'OK.' He pats a large soft bag of purple and green, string-handled, spilling a patch of faded blue. This day he wears a summer weight suit, a light coloured trilby and sandals with socks. My mother's cardigan is ruby red, with patterned frock, her hair swept back. We take the train. Fish paste sandwiches come out of his bag, a flask of tea. Moves close to my mother. They kiss, and lipstick's smudged on his stubbly pale face. This is the day when from the large bag come smaller white crumpled ones, stamped 'Lucky Bag'. I get a frog, a sherbert lemon, my brother a disguise. False nose and glasses, we swap them round.

This is the day we lose ourselves in sand. Wet, dry, we lie in it, dig, throw it over each other. The sea's on the turn, exposing the rocks. We prize off limpets, attach them to lines; crabs cling on to land in our bucket. Twenty three later, we throw them all back.

This is the day we head to a pub. My brother and I sit outside with outsize ice creams, fluffy with air. We all go for a walk, her fingers sea-clammy, smelling of Woodbines. She presses her palm into the centre of mine.

This is the day the evening comes down quick, and shadows appear. 'When's the last train?' Her face harbours old things; time, washing of uniforms, meals she can make from almost nothing. Neighbours who twitch and gossip behind curtains. But this day is his. He's grand with goodwill and beer and fears not a soul. Today. We give this day to him, as all round a crowd gathers, scents something about to happen. He undoes the bag, and pulls out clothes.

And on this beach, it's right this day as for the first and only time, with country and western suit, gangster tie, bell bottoms, he sings to us.

## Tap Roots

On the day that Seamus gets the Nobel Prize
and poetry's on the front page,
I hear his brother on the radio.
Back on the farm, tap roots sink deep.
'Och, Seamus doesn't change.
He goes to all the funerals and wakes,
and he drives an old car – it blew a gasket sure,
coming over the hill, last time he was home'.

The day after Bloody Sunday, we're in a tutorial,
English department, Queens,
and glamorous Jane from Andersonstown
with a Protestant boyfriend from the Newtonards Road
is telling us about the march. 'We thought it safer
to meet in Derry. Too dangerous in Belfast, sure.'
Heaney abandons Joyce, holds his head in his hands.
Jane says she doesn't hate the soldiers,
not the ones who pull the trigger, but others, higher.
We speak of layers in the conflict,
imagine straw, rock, clay separating into humus.
Ash Wednesday comes early that year.
Catholic students daub ash on their foreheads.

So when Heaney gets the prize, I want to shout,
use my own words. But there are layers,
mongrel words. Hybrid stock spliced north and south.
'Bloody great.' 'Wonderful.' 'Flamin' marvellous.'
His brother says, 'Och, Seamus, that's grand.'

## Breakwater

That week you caught 102 crabs,
line baited with kidneys and bacon
and gelatinous limpets you prized off rocks,
you rose at 7.30, took up position on the slipway.
Up the beach, a dead white shark floated in a pool.
Your sister threw stones at it, 'to make it come alive.'
Easy to make friends:
Americans with padded waistcoats and pony tails,
giggling Japanese girls who cocked their ears
at the local accent.The tide pulled you back
when we dragged you off that evening
for hot chips by the fire.
There were shrimps in your bucket
and edible crabs, furry and small.

Back home, still with the sea in our nostrils,
you show me a new skill: roll up newspaper,
place in letterbox, wait for dog's teeth.
'Thirty nine here, he takes the Guardian.
The Independent's up the hill.'
Your head levels with my shoulder,
three inches taller than the beginning
of summer. You're still on my lee side,
but there's a splintering of bones. And a wind.
'...drumset. Only £600. In half a year I can save...'
Battens loosen and creak,
as something encroaches like the sea.

## The Sandwich

She keeps a noose in the drawer,
and chloroform she stole from the chemists,
'just in case.' The exact number of tablets
that would kill her. She balances on the edge
of tube platforms, waiting for the whoosh of the train.
When the house is empty, she puts the noose
round her neck. Cold against her skin.
Sometimes she stands on a chair. Once she nearly slipped.

Silence she fills up with music, empty space with flowers.
There are bits sandwiched in between, like mastic.

## *Still Life*

One talks too much and waves her arms about.
No rings. No dress sense. Clothes slung together,
skirt riding up, hairy legs. Shirt – you couldn't call it white –
stain down the front, buttons missing.
Over forty and it's not even ironed.
Two coffees says her friend, but the machine's broken,
I have to make it by hand.

Sometimes I get a chance to look at the paintings.
My favourite's the dog in the kennel:
early C19th, minor painter, rumoured to be from the North.
Trendies from the Art School hardly give it a glance.
It sits, great eyes waiting, wanting to break out.

Back in the kitchen, Justin's playing 'Pussy Control'.
A man with fat arms orders a gateau. I put
potatoes in the microwave, pears on the plate,
pick up a sketchbook. Still afternoon. C18th Flemish.

Those two are still talking. Outside the gallery
the sun makes me flinch. Even the air is warm.
I press a button on a giant football. Vera Duckworth twangs on
about men with sweaty crotches. And I'm off, out of this place.

## *Names*

I come home from a group where we've argued
about using names like Wayne and Darren
when writing about the inner city, whether these names
carry too much baggage, to find Cian in bed,
middle of the afternoon. 'Wayne beat me up
and then Darren and his mates kicked me in the ribs.'
I could lift up a bus, want to kill. 'How did it start?'
'I called Wayne a dickhead. Nam kicked the hardest.
Anthony tried to stop it.' 'Is Nam Wayne's friend?'
'No, he thinks Wayne is a dickhead.' Outside,
on the wall, only Anthony meets my eyes. 'I tried to stop it'.
I am my mother at the gate of my childhood.
'You load of cowards, all you lot onto one.'
Wayne, skinny as a coathanger: 'It wasn't just me.'
His father, toothless, cheekless,
unrolls a belt, drags Wayne inside.
'Why did you call him a dickhead?' I scream at Cian,
as a bruise slowly ripens on his chin.

## Other Things

His solution: buy the biggest bottle of Prioderm.
Fifteen pounds to cover the family.
Active ingredient Carbaryl. Or take half a day off work,
queue at Spencer Place clinic for free lotion.
They insist on a live head.

A different approach: lie on bed, put on BB King,
stock up on Chandler. With a strong stomach
you can even have a sandwich.
Section the wet hair, lay it out on the pillow, go through
strand by strand, cracking the black rimmed eggs,
throwing the dead onto white paper.

A man on the radio says we have to make this lice busting
'part of a family ritual'. Like watching Casualty
with take away pizza. When I tell Andrew
to go through my head, he is pleased, says lice
always lead to sex. He doesn't know how women talk.
'Got a dirty head that one. Don't play with her.'
Doesn't know that when discussing lice in public
there are things you are allowed to say.
Like 'Isn't the lotion expensive?'
and 'It's terrible how they keep catching them.'

But you're not allowed to admit you sent them to school
without checking, that at quarter to nine,
as you were doing their hair, a fat one
caught between the teeth of your comb.
You put it out of your mind
along with bed bugs, rats, foot and mouth – other things.

# View of the Pond

Case no 564. Nine year old with bruises on buttocks.
Mother claimed fell out of go kart.
When asked to produce go kart, said
'broken'.

Perch, dab, flounder. Bream, chub, great crested newt.
Black buds. Orange tipped butterflies.
Too early.

Case no 482. Twins, four years old.
One thriving, doing well at nursery, other pale, withdrawn.
Unexplained marks on back – cigarette burns?
Bad teeth.

Fancy tailed goldfish. Hedgehogs emerging from dead leaves.
Pondweed and water lilies, frogbits and fairy moss.
Sludge.

Case no 483. Twelve year old carer, missed four months school.
Mother has MS. Half eaten tins of dog food on the floor.
Phone hospital. Girl alone. Aunty coming.
Manchester.

Washing line, a trike, a swing, roller skates.
Next door's high fence.
They didn't speak for months.

Case no 602. Baby covered in nappy rash.
Clean needle scheme ended. Methadone.
Partner dead.

Beyond the pond, fields before Chester,
and the horse that sat on Liam once.
Frost weakens, view
clear.

## *To My Mother*

### *(after Iain Crichton Smith's 'to my mother')*

You were packing margarine tubs in Liverpool, and the pale yellow liquid hardens and swirls like chocolate. Mist rises from far out at sea and in the factory fish fingers are dropping, and the liquid so hot it burnt your fingers so that the tips were scarred red and your lipstick crumbles at the corner of your mouth.

I was in Belfast studying and the anthropology books were on my table, and the Russian dictionary on my shelf and I drinking Guinness in the student bar, after walking round cairns for the feel of the landscape. Snug in university squares, with elm trees, soft rain in the background, an occasional shot or explosion, we soon drowned it out.

Sadness is covering me because you did not have my chances and because of the way things were then. Although 'cleverest' and 'most popular', you could not get away. You bore eight of us and each time it grew harder until the final babies were dragged out of you, small as rats. I would not like to be plunging my hands up chickens or laying out fish fingers to the distant hum of motorway traffic, then the children wailing late into the night, and your bones so weary to drag up the stairs.

Though I might weep in my writing, they are my own marks I am making and as well as a crib for my hopes, I have a typewriter and the echo of others' voices as I bounce my words out into the dark.

## *Funeral at Easter*

When the funeral director asks me what date my father died
I say Palm Sunday. We go through the arrangements:
pine coffin or oak, white or pink satin lining.
Will the body lie at home? When should he call round?
How many cars do we want? Flowers or not?
I stave him off by crying. I give a good impression of grief.
I wonder briefly what we could put in the coffin. Stones.
A dead pig. He does not push. 'Closed casket or open?' he asks,
after a decent interval. 'Oh, closed,' I say quickly.
The decay will be awful. 'There are things we can do.'
He mentions makeup and hairwashing.
'Was it a sudden death? An accident?
If you don't want to see him, you don't have to.
It's entirely up to you.' 'Pink satin,' I tell him and 'Yes,
I do want to see him. No, it wasn't sudden.'
Twenty five years. Only now I want to bury him,
smell death, run my fingers through it, know he's gone.

## No More

No more Ridley Road cream cheese bagels at two in the morning. No more cheap Mondays at the Rio: Cafe Direct coffee, discounts for wheelchair users 'and their carers'. No more parent and toddler groups, riding along the canal past the 'No Cycling' signs, emerging at Vicky Park, seeing the herded deer, you sticking your fingers through wire, bitten by an East End chicken. No more grey stone dogs, no more freewheeling down the hill to Old Ford lock. No more cabbage in Pellicis, no more cobbles along the Market Porters' route to the City, the back way to the British Library, the sour smell of the canal, no more gods at the Hackney Empire, no more swimming in Clapton baths, or Whiston Road warm slipper baths, before we got a bathroom; Chinese men on a Monday, the waiting room with mother in law's tongue. No more Centeprise tuna fish rolls, or Greek salty olives, flat bread, halva, bloody chickens hanging in the market.

## *Two Cappuccino and a Tuna Fish Sandwich*

The day the Guildford Four were granted their appeal,
there was blood in my knickers
and you told me you were pregnant
as we walked down Gower Street.
(Two cappuccino and a tuna fish sandwich.)
Carole Richardson, inside fourteen years,
wants children, I, outside in the bare treed winter sun,
and Japanese tourists by the British Museum,
want children. The mildest winter for years. I hold your arm,
protective suddenly. Two tickets to an afternoon film.
Only three o'clock and we've cried already.

*Internet*

A cave painting is found in the Ardeche,
while the tree dwellers of Lancashire,
seventy foot up, clamber along walkways in the sky.
Cattle, bison, horses on walls in La Grotte Chavet.
In Stanworth Valley wood, ropes web,
bright colours woven in. 'It's like being at sea,'
says one girl. 'No one's fallen out yet.'
They eat rice and soybeans. Down below,
yellow diggers move closer, then stop, the incline too steep.
The road firm agree they'll have to use horses
to plough up the earth. Deep in French caves,
horses pause, hooves at the ready. We dare not exhale,
knowing the breath in our bodies can destroy them.

## Creating

Do you believe in God?' The man sits next to me
on the bus. There are plenty of spare seats.
'No.' He smells of wet raincoat,
there are gaps in his teeth. 'I'll pray for you,
I feel sorry for you. How can there not be a god?
How can all this ...? the trees and the plants ...?'
His arms widen as a warehouse slips past.
'And us – all come out of nothing?
It can't.' A pain in my shoulder moves up to my neck.
'There must be a god. I mean – look at you –
your left knee is perfect, your right knee is perfect.'
He touches my leg. 'Terrible,' he goes on.
'All these young women getting pregnant.
'Not right. Parasites, living off the country.
By the way, what's your job? Do you work?'
I want to knee him with my perfect knees.
'You mustn't work or you'd say. I bet you're a single
parent, a parasite. I'll pray for you, bloody skiver.
God's watching, you know.' There's a twinge in my head
as he picks up his stick, limps down the bus.
Heads turn as words float like a prayer –
'... disgusting ... bloody skiver ... single parent...'
'Was he bothering you, flower?' asks the driver.

## Umbrellas

She dreams of umbrellas filled with sweets
and her childhood in Andaluciá, the fiesta,
when giant men on stilts unleash firecrackers
and figures are burnt, tomatoes thrown, the streets fill with water.
When she lifts her large black English umbrella
raindrops big as sweets plop in.
She crouches by a radiator. Everything is shadow.
When she woke that first October sunrise,
the clock said it was morning.
All day she held up her face to the sky,
searching for the sun.

## *Dun Laoghaire*

Glass in her bed.
The Pope is in Ireland this summer
when we meet Ainé on the road,
us straight off the Holyhead boat,
mist in the air, a promise of sun,
cycles laden with bags and my child.

Ainé invites us for breakfast and bed.
Unwilling, we agree: pan toast, stewed tea.
My child wants to sleep. But there's glass in the bed,
scattered in bedclothes,  so he lies on the floor,
catches the sun in a necklace.
Aine picks up a sugar lump
of underwired glass, drops it back down.
'Last night they knocked the window in.'
Her blouse comes apart. Like something unconnected,
she pushes a breast back in. Then we're off up the coast road,
past Italian style palm trees. My son pokes his head
through the folds of my skirt. 'You look like a rainbow.'
A woman at the campsite says no, she has not seen the Pope.

## *When we moved from London,*

                    we had to leave things behind.
Kitchen stuff, a vacuum cleaner nozzle, a frying pan,
spoons. My son hopped to Leeds with one shoe.
It was that jumper we found later, the one we'd argued over,
in a friend's garden. Straw, paper, hairless dead baby mouse.
Rows about sizes and colours. He'd not wanted Woolworths,
dreamt of Ellesse. Not the right shade. Like us, dreaming.
We wanted wallpaper, in the houses that we moved to.
Always getting to the stage of stripping and taking off,
never reaching the next point where you put something back on.

## Going Home

February, her shrunken in bed. 'Home' and then 'mother'; to clutch at the roots of the words. *Susan Smith, Tommy Dacey, Tommy Grindley, Linda Brogan. Biz, Diane who started her periods before everyone else. Libby. Cracko. Drains, McIlveney, the Mackas who lived down the street. Eileen O'Brien, whose Billy worked on the lorries. The girl from the mobile who sold loosies. Albert who walked the pub each night before his leg gave way from under him.*

March. 'I'm leaving,' she mouths, 'I'm pushing the boat out.' In her bungalow with carpets and central heating, she gives me photos. On the wall, seven of us stare out. The room fills with objects. 'They've blown up the old flats,' she tells me. Dust where she lived.

Too late. To visit the past when she can no longer hear me. 'Did you know?' shout my sisters. 'Have you heard?' We play games, after flights to the north and the south, further onto Europe and the States. Her children spread, following invisible arrows, the smell of the sea.

April. A little more stooped, her eyes becoming rheumy. Passes round cakes. Calls me Meg. To rake up the past: *Mary, good at art, left school pregnant – '24 years. I've never been happy. He drinks.' Liz, with me in the Chicken Roast the night my father died, Linda, who went off to art college and married an Italian, Jackie who heads a school, Ida who died of cancer of the cervix, Sheila who had a heart attack, Janet whose son was born without arms.*

My mother's preparing for the end. Eats by herself. Says she's got £1,000 'in case anything happens'. In my dreams, I see overhead railways; my father carrying bananas, great liners leaving for America, the West Indies. 'To Ireland', says a sign. Gradually her bones break back towards the river. Not far, this route to the shore.

May. At the Pier Head, empty of boats, she, leaning on our arms, waves like a queen. There's a wind which whips our clothes, rain squalls off the sea. We sniff to smell the sweat of men who shifted bales, keen our ears to hear the noise of anchors drop, but the river's quiet and empty now. She touches her face where her ear used to be, leans towards the water, scouring for a boat. But the river's quiet and empty now. Not long.

'I want to go home now,' she says. 'I want to go home.'

## Nearly There

Afternoon of Sport's Day, third day of the heatwave.
In a field behind the Civil Service Club,
benches line up like pews. Dry grass scratches my legs.

A teacher fills plastic with orange. The obstacle race:
my daughter's slow off the mark,
looking backwards for my face.
On the outside, a small grim boy

ducks and wriggles to the line. 'Nearly there,' I shout,
while the sun burns my arm and parents stagger back
after a 'Sports Day Special'. 'You did really well.'
'I came last.'

Victors return, cheeks stuffed with sweets.
I offer water. Last race. Older boys show loss in the face.
Yellowed leaves hardly move. Magpies squabble.
And I'm watching her. Reception, 2A, 3A, 4,
Years 7, 11. Outwards, running.
Rockall, Mallin, Finisterre.
The craters of the moon.

## *Differences*

he speaks to me of other things
like cracks in the wall
and spills on the floor
and I've lost a plastic spoon this week
and somebody left the fridge door open
and the ice all melted

(the potatoes were raw tonight
like the fish
I'd set the oven
forgot to light it)

my face creases     I cry at the sink
I do not believe this mountain I live with
I want to talk of other things
like death and life
and the failure of post-war planning
and how can we go on together
like this

and he says let's make the shelves
let's pretend
let's play at house
mummies and daddies

happy
together

## *To Phil (if he wakes up)*

Anger
Anger drove me to it
I killed him at last
one night when we were alone in the house
And the stage was set for sex
and romance
and he fell asleep
smelling of creosote and beer.
So I killed him. It was simple really
with a knife I had from the Guides.
It was sharp and strong.
So I found his heart and looked at him sleeping and unaware
He'd always said he wanted to die in his sleep
the irony was good
I smiled at him once and the knife slid in,
meeting resistance at first
and then something that felt like gristle
under my butcher's knife in the kitchen
He looked up once
and his eyes had that wide open
slightly surprised look
just before he came
and his tongue hung out like it always did.